THE
MOON
IS ALWAYS
ROUND

BY JONATHAN GIBSON

ILLUSTRATED BY JOE HOX

New Growth Press, Greensboro, NC 27401
newgrowthpress.com
Text copyright © 2019 by Jonathan Gibson
Illustration copyright © 2019 by New Growth Press

Interior Design and Typesetting: Trish Mahoney, themahoney.com
Cover/Interior Illustrations: Joe Hox

Thanks to Nate Morgan-Locke for help with the narrative structure.

ISBN: 978-1-64507-027-6

Library of Congress Control Number: 2019945517

Printed in India

29 28 27 26 25 24 23 22   6 7 8 9 10

Ben,

Whatever happens in life, remember:
The moon is round.
The moon is always round.

I love you.
Dad

When I look up on a sunny day, the sky is blue and bright, and jet planes paint white lines on its canvas.

When I look up on a stormy day,
the sky is grey and dull,
and clouds pour rain,

and **flash** and **boom** with lightning and thunder.

When I look up on a summer's evening,
the sky is red and orange and purply pink,

and the sun looks like it's falling from the sky, on fire.

When I look up on a clear night, the sky is dark, and the stars **twinkle** and **sparkle** like diamonds…

But the moon isn't always round.

Dad said,

"The moon is always round,

even when you can't see all of it."

When Dad told me that I was getting a little sister,

the moon looked like a banana.

But Dad said,
"The moon is always round."

When the crib was put together,
the moon looked like a slice of apple.

But Dad said,

"The moon is always round."

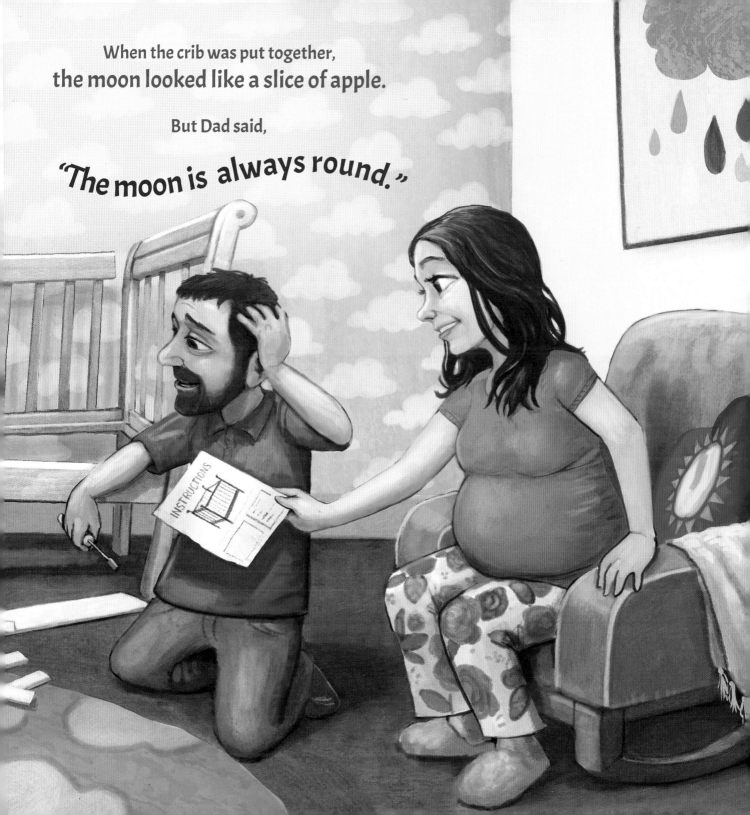

When mummy's tummy began
to look like a watermelon,

the moon looked like
a shriveled orange.

But Dad said,

"The moon is
always round."

Even when I was told that my little sister
wasn't coming to live with us after all the waiting,

Dad said,
**"The moon is
always round."**

When my parents left in the middle of the night for the hospital,
and the next morning I went off to pre-school,

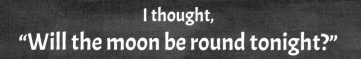
I thought,
"Will the moon be round tonight?"

Dad said,
"The moon is always round."

And he replied,
"I don't know why.
But the moon is always round."

When we got home from the hospital,
I looked for the moon before bed . . .

it was a half-moon!

But Dad said,

"The moon is always round."

And when it was still just the three of us,
and we went to the church to say good-bye,

my Dad asked me,
"What shape is the moon?"

I said,
"The moon is always round."

And Dad said,
"What does
that mean?"

"For the LORD is good;
his steadfast love endures forever,
and his faithfulness to all generations."

Psalm 100:5

Lessons for Children

The Moon

Ask your child(ren) to look in the book to see in how many shapes the moon appears.

The moon serves as a good illustration to teach our child(ren) about God's goodness. Even when we cannot see the whole moon as it orbits the earth, the moon is always round. It's the same with God's goodness. There are times in our lives when things happen to us that make us question or doubt God's goodness, like when someone in our family dies. But just because we cannot always see God's goodness during difficult times, this does not mean that God is not good in those times. God is always good, even when we cannot see it, just like the moon is always round, even when we cannot see all of it.

Memory verse:

"For the Lord is good; his steadfast love endures forever, and his faithfulness to all generations." (Psalm 100:5)

Good Friday

Ask your child(ren) to look in the book to see how many crosses they can find. (There are 10).

Good Friday is a concrete example to teach our child(ren) about God's goodness in difficult times. On Good Friday, when Jesus died on the cross, he experienced the most difficult of times. That day, the sun was blanked out and the whole world went dark—the darkest it has ever been. No stars twinkled. There was not even a sliver of the moon in the sky to give Jesus some light. And yet in the darkness, God showed the whole world that he was still good. Because in that moment, Jesus died for our sins, so that we could be forgiven. It's why the day is called "Good Friday," because even though Jesus died in the darkness, God was still good—just like the moon was still round, even though no one could see it.

Memory verse:

"In him [Jesus], we have redemption through his blood, the forgiveness of sins, in accordance with the riches of his grace." (Ephesians 1:7)

The Story behind This Book[1]

When our son Benjamin was about three-years old, I held him up to the window one evening and he pointed to the moon.

"Look. The moon!" he said.

It was a crescent moon. I explained to him that the moon could appear in different shapes, but the moon was always round. From that, I developed a simple catechism for him.

Q. Ben, what shape is the moon tonight?

A. The moon is a crescent moon, or a half-moon, or a gibbous moon, or a full moon.

Q. What shape is the moon always?

A. The moon is always round.

Q. What does that mean?

A. God is always good.

Little did I know that, even as a three-year old, the catechism would soon become so very important in his life. Sometime later, on March 13, 2016, his younger sister, Leila Judith Grace, died at 39 weeks in her mother's womb. Four days later, she was stillborn at 10:25am on March, 17, 2016. Ben came to meet her in the hospital later that afternoon. He gave her "Bazza" the giraffe as a gift. He held her, and then a few hours later, he said goodbye to her.

As I drove him home that night, he asked, "Daddy, will mummy ever grow a baby that wakes up?"

I told him I didn't know.

He asked, "Why isn't Leila coming home with us?"

I told him because she's gone to be with Jesus.

He asked, "Why has she gone to be with Jesus?"

I told him because Jesus called her name and she went to him.

He asked, "Will Leila come to us after a day with Jesus in heaven?"

I told him that when you meet Jesus, you don't want to go anywhere else.

He asked, "Why?"

I told him because he is such a wonderful person.

He asked, "Does Leila not like us?"

I told him that she does like us, she just likes Jesus more.

He asked again, "But why is Leila not coming home with us?"

I said, "Ben, I don't really know why."

And then I recalled our catechism, so I started to talk to him about the moon. We talked about how sometimes when we look up at the moon, we can only see a crescent moon or a half-moon or a gibbous moon.

And then I asked him, "What shape is the moon, Ben?"

"The moon is always round," he replied.

I said, "What does that mean?"

He said, "God is always good."

"That's right," I replied, and drove on in silence, tears streaming down my face.

That night after I tucked Ben into bed and left him under the care of a close friend, I went back to the hospital to be with Jackie and Leila. Just before I got into the car, I looked up to see if there was a moon in the night sky. There was—a half-moon! That captured exactly how Jackie and I felt. We couldn't see the whole of God's goodness because Leila was dead. But we knew that the moon was round, even though we couldn't see all of it. The moon is always round.

A few weeks later we held a funeral service for Leila. I gave a eulogy for her, and at the end I addressed Ben. I told him that as he grows up, he may have questions about why Leila died, but I wanted him to remember what he had learnt about the moon. I asked him again in the service, "What shape is the moon, Ben?"

"The moon is always round," he replied.

I said, "What does that mean?"

He said, "God is always good."

Out of the mouth of babes and infants God has ordained praise (Psalm 8:2).

Since then, the moon has become so meaningful to our family. Ben has a picture of the moon above his bed. Five simple words curve below the moon: "The moon is always round." We pray that our story, and the story of Jesus on the cross, points others (of all ages) to the goodness of God, even in the darkness.

---

[1] My inspiration for the illustration about the moon was gleaned from the story of a young Christian girl who died of cancer at fourteen years old. After she died, her journal was discovered by family and friends. In the middle of it was an index card that simply read: "The moon is round." See Bryan Chapell, *The Hardest Sermons You'll Ever Have to Preach: Help from Trusted Preachers for Tragic Times* (Grand Rapids: Zondervan, 2011), 112.

A Catechism on the Moon

Q1. What shape is the moon tonight?

A1. The moon is a crescent moon, or a half-moon, or a gibbous moon, or a full moon.

Q2. What shape is the moon always?

A2. The moon is always round.

Q3. What does it mean that the moon is always round?

A3. God is always good.

Q4. How do you know that God is always good?

A4. Because of Good Friday.

Q5. What happened on Good Friday?

A5. In the darkness God's Son Jesus died for our sins, so that we could be forgiven.

Q6. What Bible verse teaches us that God is always good?

A6. Psalm 100:5: "For the Lord is good; his steadfast love endures forever, and his faithfulness to all generations."